ANTHOLOG

POEMS '70

Poems '70

Editor
Wyn Binding

GWASG GOMER
LLANDYSUL
1970

First Impression - July 1970

© GWASG GOMER, LLANDYSUL

*This Anthology is published with the
support of the Welsh Arts Council*

PRINTED BY J. D. LEWIS AND SONS LTD.
GWASG GOMER, LLANDYSUL

CONTENTS

FOREWORD

This is a selection of poems by Welsh writers which I have enjoyed reading during the past year. Some are published for the first time, but many are from magazines published in Wales. I have included some of the verses submitted to the Welsh Arts Council's Dial-a-Poem service—I hope they encourage you to dial Cardiff 45144. I have also included some poems from books by Emyr Humphreys, John Ormond, Sally Roberts and Harri Webb which have been published by Welsh presses. One book by David Jones has especially excited me. But *The Tribune's Visitation* published by the Fulcrum Press, London, is one poem and cannot be justly represented by a selected passage. It is a fine achievement.

Acknowledgments are due to the editors and publishers of *The Anglo-Welsh Review, The London Welshman, Mabon* and *Poetry Wales*, in which some of the poems in this anthology have appeared ; to Christopher Davies for two poems from *Requiem and Celebration* by John Ormond ; to Gwasg Gee for three poems from *Ancestor Worship* by Emyr Humphreys ; to Gwasg Gomer for three poems from *Turning Away* by Sally Roberts and two poems from *The Green Desert* by Harri Webb.

June 1970   WYN BINDING

1. *Pan Fo'r Gwynt*

Pan fo'r gwynt yn wyrdd,
Gwymon yn y môr,
Cnawd yr eiddew,
A gwydrau ffenestri'r llyn.

Pan fo'r gwynt yn felyn,
Y tywod a'r cregyn,
Corawdau'r daffodil,
A'r lleuad ar lawr y llyn.

Pan fo'r gwynt yn goch
Ymhell ar y môr,
Ceirch ac afalau,
A thanau'n cynnau yn y llyn.

A phan fo'r gwynt yn ddu,
A'r haul ynghudd
Yn seleri'r llyn,
Caf hyd i'r peth a gollwyd.

Euros Bowen

1. *When the Wind*

When the wind is green,
Seaweed and sea,
Ivy flesh,
And the lake's window panes.

When the wind is coloured yellow,
The sand and the sea-shells,
The daffodil's choruses,
And the moon low in the lake.

When the wind reddens
Far out on the sea,
Oats and apples,
And fires alight in the lake.

And when the wind darkens,
And the sun is concealed
In the lake's cellars,
I shall find again what I have lost.

The four colours mentioned are colours in nature at different times of the year. The "lake's cellars" is an image representing the memory of something thought of as lost. But this memory associated with brighter seasons returns in the blackness of winter.

So the structure of the poem combines two aspects of memory—conscious memory, the memory of the colours on the surface of the lake and instances of colour associations, and unconscious memory, where what is lost is retained, although hidden, hidden in "the lake's cellars". In poetry we combine both memories.

2. *Bread of Heaven*

Huw Edwards, quarryman.
Granite hard of hand and lung,
Coughs behind the hymn-book,
Tonic-solfa, of course—
Brought up by Jones the School
On Curwen's modulator—
Tries to dust his throat :
Must pitch it right,
No organist this morning.
Difficulty with the dust
So coughs again.
Difficulty with that awkward slab
On the rock-face last week too.
The dust came from the rock.
Rock is daily bread.
Dust is cough
Again—that's it !
The chapel walls resound—
' Feed me now and evermore.'

3. Sea-View

Suspended on the rock-face
A thousand feet above the twice-a-day
Washerwoman, landwife sea,
Huw Edwards looks out to Great Orme's head
Round which the Wyrm-proud
Longships from the North
Savaged the waves in violent search
For anchorage in Conway bay.
His tired, brown eyes
Cannot see into the murderous past
When wild Odin screamed for blood
As horned death leapt upon Welsh sand.
Huw sees only the distant speck on noontide gold,
Approaching, autumnal, to harvest his sweat
In the throbbing barn of its hold.

4. *The Garden*

Coming back to the garden
After a growth of years
I am aware of its sameness ;
All is in place, but smaller
Now that I am man-tall over
The jungle of beans, curly kail
And the clustered bright mass
Of dahlias bursting in the sun.
The wood of the fences,
The leaning trestles around the lawn,
These still stand their brows greening
And flaked by the worrying seasons :
I had not thought them such a colour
Nor the lawn and its apple-tree to be so small.
The clear lake of sailing boats puff-blown
Is a clouded rain-barrel
Rusting now in its usefulness
Leaving me to stare back at myself in its water.

5. *After the Match*

After the match we returned
mud-hot and exultant
to the mine, moribund
with its hollow aura of breath.
We showered in tiled cubicles,
a white paradox here ;
our pleasure-mud mocking
the dust of years.
Then beer and bingo unwinding
of the clubhouse : yet the singing
was a self-parody.
An old man worked his way
through the glass-arms almost unnoticed ;
a cloth-cap and neck-scarf
framing the past.
The valley will soon know
little of such faces
conquered by the black grime.
Grandad's wet-stare
into the fire-place glow
conjuring of red and black coals
past work-mates there,
bound in one life
by the black and green slopes.
The slopes are crossed.

6. *Portrait of Auntie Blodwen*

Women who were mothers told us about it,
chicks hatching in Auntie Blodwen's,
go and watch, Auntie will be pleased.

Once we heard, Poor Blodwen, he
gives her hell, heard and did not hear,
but the silence after the warning nod
told of the acid dropped by mischance
in ears too young for such chemistry.
Uncomprehending, we guessed only
an image endangered, that Blodwen was different.

Her house still stands, roofed and occupied
by others in its sovereign now, mocking
its dusky pitiful remnants of rooms
and gestures and moments waiting under
memory's curtains for their last appearances.
At her house where the lino, the brass and the furniture
but never the faces shone, where we never
went round the side but knocked on the door,
were the eggs on a tray in front of the fire.
On our knees we laughed at the small explosions,
the fierce unseen thrusting in shells,
the pauses for rest or thought of life
the size of an eggcup breaking into the light.

Aunt Blodwen stands there, stands for as long
as my ever will last, never did never will
sit in her house, lost fingers
stroking the tablecloth, watching
us newly broken from darkness laugh
at the chicks, and her drowning smile floats
in the waters of her face, hurt by the light.

7. *Shalom*

Amnon, Gideon, Shimon,
where are you now ?
Practising precision ?
I taught you how.

Joel, Giora, David,
what are you at ?
Taking the line's full sweep ?
I taught you that.

Daniel, Ilan, Elisha,
what is your task ?
Interrogation ?
I taught you to ask.

Rachel, Nourith, Yael,
what do you do ?
Reject the sentimental ?
I taught that too.

O children of Israel,
my pupils once
in a Dutch oasis,
genius and dunce,

what have I taught you,
what will grow next
from those tranquil mornings
at work on a text ?

But I send my greeting ;
for what I heard
grow through those lines
was this green word.

8. *Ancestors*

William Oliver maker
of winnowing machines, John Wood
labourer, in the fields of
the eighteenth century. You are good
forefathers for a man to have.
You might have understood

my making with words, my zest
for earth and spade. William Beere
tea merchant, savouring the joke.
And William Garlick, pioneer
of that name in Wales, who long
ago committed me here.

But of them all, the humble names
in the registers, I think of you
Nicholas Garlick, martyr,
and Derby Bridge your rendezvous,
in the armada year, with light.
You were an extremist too.

9. *Ieuan ap Hywel Swrdwal*

Swrdwal, you are
our ancestor, the arch-poet
of those who write
in English, did they know it.

What was it like,
that Oxford of new gables,
honey-coloured walls,
in which you turned the tables?

Even the calm
Virgin, her griefs forgotten,
must have smiled to see
a literature begotten.

You sang for her,
threw the English your laughter.
I still hear it
five centuries after.

10. *Ancestor Worship*

1. The dead are horizontal and motionless
    They take less room
    Than the stones which mark the tomb

    But the words they spoke
    Grow like flowers in the cracked rock

    Their ghosts move easily between words
    As people move between trees
    Gathering days and sunlight
    Like fuel for an invisible fire.

2. Grandparents whose portraits hang
    Like ikons in our hearts
    Carved out acres drew up codicils
    To brace our lives
    But the new estates cover the fields
    All the names are changed and their will
    Is broken up by sewers and pylons.

3. Our remote ancestors knew better.
    They were all poets
    They all wove
    Syllabic love into their wooden homes

    They saw the first invaders come
    Pushing their boats through the water meadows
    Their teeth and their swords glittering in the stealthy light
    And they carved metrical systems out of their own flesh.

4. The air is still committed to their speech
   Their voices live in the air
   Like leaves like clouds like rain
   Their words call out to be spoken
   Until the language dies
   Until the ocean changes.

11. *A Democratic Vista*

Strange sanctuary this, perched on the rising cornstack
Like a desert saint on a broken pillar
Staring, eyes unstirring until hill field sea are one
The procession of thought blurred
Into the regular rising and falling of a sinewy arm
And the dry rustle of sheaves.
Tom Williams, Guto, Dick Williams, Wil bach, Dafydd Dew and
        me,
We are the people ; our conversation is smooth and superficial
Like a veneer of grained wood, curves leading nowhere
Which was where they started.
We are the people, for whom politicians shout and soldiers fight
We sow and reap, eat and sleep, copulate in secret, think
In circumferences of one dimension.
We are the sacred people, the secular mystery, the host,
Whitman's elastic deity, Marx's material, Rousseau's noble savage
Mayakovsky's beloved—
Tom, Guto, Dic, Wil, Dafie, and me—
Reasonably efficient between dawn and sunset,
God chewing tobacco, God drinking tea, digesting rice.
We are the people.
God is not mocked.

12. *From Father to Son*

There is no limit to the number of times
Your father can come to life, and he is as tender as ever he was
And as poor, his overcoat buttoned to the throat,
His face blue from the wind that always blows in the outer dark-
ness
He comes towards you, hesitant,
Unwilling to intrude and yet driven at the point of love
To this encounter.

You may think
That love is all that is left of him, but when he comes
He comes with all his winters and all his wounds.
He stands shivering in the empty street,
Cold and worn like a tramp at the end of a journey
And yet a shape of unquestioning love that you
Uneasy and hesitant of the cold touch of death
Must embrace.

Then, before you can touch him
He is gone, leaving on your fingers
A little more of his weariness
A little more of his love.

13. *Lament*

(Reflection after the first one man exhibition at the New Art Centre, London)

There has been
A one man show,
A man on show,
The rectangles of his mind
Set out along a long wall
Trying to live
In the West End.
West Wales Icons,
Thought up,
Felt up,
In a second story flat
Above Carmarthen.
Walls and Stones
And Celtic Crosses
Personalised in paint
And powdered metal.
Marks made by
Liverpool and Wales
On canvas and board
Framed in aluminium
Against a hessian wall.
They clung together,
Speaking Anglo-Welsh
In low tones,

The ponderous shapes,
Scratched and scored
Balanced precisely
In golden splendour,
And were not disturbed
By the precisely balanced
Judgements of the clientele
Who looked
But did not buy
They looked but
Did not buy
Did not buy,
They
Did
Not
Buy.

14. *Incident*

The lecturer,
His two small children
And I, carrying a live cock
And a bucket
Trooped to the wood,
In the dusk,
A practical demonstration
Was to follow
On killing a bird
For the pot.
In a clearing
Flanked by trees
(Which rustled like my heart)
The bird was placed
Head resting on a stump.
Jac handed me a cleaver
Saying ' Hit it hard '
I looked at
The interested innocence
Of the children,
The rose pink sky,
But not at the bird.
And hit it hard.

The head stayed :
The bird struggled :
The children looked :

The pupil felt ashamed
And hit.
And hit
At the neck,
Which would not cut,
Until it did.

Jac said ' good '
The children picked flowers
And leaves with fluid ease.
The bird was put
In the bucket
And the three of them
And I
Walked to the house.

15. *Communication*

Play at words
appraise   confess
consult   admit
communicate

Keep in touch
call meetings
give orders   make requests
end silence
end   silence
To avoid futile
misconception
and fantasy
cultivate
precise
words
and
use
sound
as Bach
developed
the counter
subject in an
intricate fugue

Words are necessary
For identity
They affirm presence
And deny absence

They come before meaning
Which is merely a
Front for expressing
Our fear of silence

16. *Sayings of an Uncle*

(For S.T.)

I

An accident he had turned him.
The old humour froze in twisted rhymes,
Pointing the way of his thoughts
Like fresh tracks in untrampled snow.

He would come out with quaint sayings,
Calling himself ' Sambo the darky '
And ' Sam the man from Penyfan. '

People sympathised, bringing themselves
As gifts and toys to please and amuse ;
And he was their child turning round and round,
Losing them, finding them, round and round.

The family distrusted him,
Knowing the comings and goings of his
Pantomime wits kept him on the dole.

II

Awake, he kept time walking between the hours
On reciprocal visits to the unsick,
Who practised replies on him and turned away.

'Toodle-oo,' he'd sing out ;
'The cosy corner kid must have air
Before he climbs the stair.'

III
Men about town made room in the park
And the library ; a place was established
For the new voice on politics, racing and sport
—Which were the true areas of talk
Before he came speaking of other things,
Saying there were 'millionaires from St. Clears'
And 'slaves in Wales.'

17. *Testament*

I cannot be sure what
I remember, but it was
Not a heroic escape, a grave
Hypocrisy strangled, the cortege
Of deacons stunned by one
Honest stroke. I was the child
Of belief, aching pitifully
In the unready hours
For the wounds I should suffer
When I walked out weaponless
And grown.

They were all heroes then,
All bullyboys kicking the pews
In, stirring their history up
In a pint-pot, jeering
The shabby, unmuscled parades
Of the old Model Army.
But I was a little trembling
Fellow who had known love
And saw only greed
And false heart in such great
Drunken tales.

They have not survived,
That swarthy cenedl, struggling out
Of the candled tallut, cousins to
Generations of sour hay, evil-looking
Apples and oatmeal porringers.
A quick incontinence of seed
Cried in the barn, a mind to spit
And squat harried the gorse
Into burning, and the melancholy
Rhos burst into plots, as circumscribed
Only as the lean muscle yearning
Carefully for love could lay
Around each house. But of that
Merely a life or two, enough to multiply
Cousins like bloodspots in the wasted
Grass. Then a new swarming, under
An aged queen, before they walked
Their milgis over the ragged hill
They ghosted every shift, farming
A memory of that last-seen
Country that was never theirs.
It was not will was lacking then
So much as instinct, a gift
Of seed for their backyard culture,
A grip on the girl who bears.

They have not survived.
Coughing in terraces above

The coal, their doorsteps whitened
And the suds of pride draining
Away down the numbered
Steps to the dole, they denied
Both past and future, willing
No further movement than the rattle
Of phlegm, a last composure
Of limb and attitude.
For this dark cousinhood only I
Can speak. Why am I unlike
Them, alive and jack in office,
Shrewd among the plunderers ?

19. *For Jenkin Jones, Prisoner at Carmarthen, these*

My sun, capricious, holds its heaven. I cannot wish you
Well of the morning, Jenkin, who would engage
For no single luminary but riddled stars
Over every common, gorse-fanged and thorn-staked
Stars that gave back fire from the Approvers' gaze
In a governable brilliance. O I could rally you, calling
You coxcomb, fool for all your port.
But as the sun rises and the old insects warm themselves
I lack the heart.

It is not solely that I am older, sick
Of my cause's rectitude in the mouths of grasshoppers.
I know now how it was that Sions Tŷ Mawr
Could be a servitor at board in my own College
Keeping a hungry distance from the gentlemen
Commoners. Already you had speech
Truculent for tapsters, stiff that bread
Should be broken with prayer and thanksgiving,
Action for creed.

Your unshot gravity was something ridiculous, though,
Captain Jenkin. That soldierly dispatch, those
Pistols always primed, the hundred men
Close in the covert and you called. Did you not
Mistake, from earliest trial, the cause you fought for ?
Was it this world to win for your soul-starved
Werin or did you faze the track in minding
Postboys and serving-men, losing the kingdom
And the king ?

What have you done for the wretched but raise
False hopes ? On Tuesday a week I rode
Under rain to the hovels above Morlais brook
Seeking to bleed a woman from distemper. A lad
Called Courage Gronow showed me a flintlock
To the breast, said that the men were off
Raising a rescue for Capten Shinkin, taken
By the ungodly. How long before they hark at the world
And waken ?

Truth is not to be cupped and portioned as you pass
The elements down the rows of the new devout.
All such equality as seems to stretch
To the here and now is gross
Misjudgment, your catabaptism a pander simply
To brutes, the gravest acceptance of room
And substance in each idiot head.
The world has put you down for it, as a practice
Ill-consideréd.

And yet I ponder. We never played together,
You and I, as boys, nor said two words
In College. But I know you roared them off,
The dogs sniffing out royalists. ' No poet ever
Sets his feet to a Parliament's measure ' was your word
Joking down the Llanddetty men who would take
Teeth to a cloak or a comfit without command.
I know : Matthew Havard told me, choking
Behind his hand.

But hard on Breda and the young king's
Homecoming there was that strange report
Of the holes in the church door at Talybont,
Your furious aim at the lock, and the dozen
Riders smoking westwards into the dark. Was this
An end, then, Jenkin, or a new aim other-wordly
Taken ? You are a friend of my doubts, an enemy
Who troubles my heart in failing. Fare
You well. H.V.

20. *At His Father's Grave*

Here lies a shoemaker whose knife and hammer
Fell idle at the height of summer,
Who was not missed so much as when the rain
Of winter brought him back to mind again.

He was no preacher but his working text
Was, 'See all dry this winter and the next.'
Stand still. Remember his two hands, his laugh,
His craftsmanship. They are his epitaph.

21. *Landscape Without Figures*

Cynddylan's hall is dark to-night,
Says the Welsh bard from the days of bows and arrows ;
The blood of kinsmen reddened some small rivers,
The singing fool left helpless as usual.

There'd been some battle or other
Fought in a bog, no doubt ; as unromantic
And merciless as ever. But fine phrases
Took in charred stones and rafters,
Dead fires under chimneys, benches overturned,
Many men dead out in the dank country.

The old poets were good at this kind of thing ;
A bit high-flown, but genuine enough ;
Cooking the metre but seldom the reaction.
I know how they felt in the evening wasteland of Wales :
I come upon a farmhouse with old stones tumbling,
The roof fallen-in, nettles at every lintel
And empty cowsheds crumbling, an elder
Loaded with berries and nobody to pick them,
No sign of blood, only tins and broken bottles,
But once lived-in, and now no longer lived-in.

The hall of somebody who was is empty to-night.
But there was a man and his house. It might be said
The elder blossoms each year in token celebration.

22. *Salmon*

(For Ceri Richards)

The river sucks them home.
The lost past claims them.
      Beyond the headland
It gropes into the channel
Of the nameless sea.
      Offshore they submit
To the cast, to the taste of it.
It releases them from salt,
Their thousand miles in odyssey
For spawning. It rehearsed their return.
      From the beginning ; now
      It clenches them like a fist.

The echo of once being here
Possesses and inclines them.
      Caught in the embrace
Of nothing that is not now,
Riding in with the tide-race,
      Not by their will,
Not by any will they know,
They turn fast to the caress
Of their only course. Sea-hazards done,
They ache towards the one world
      From which their secret
      Sprang, perpetuate

More than themselves, the ritual
Claim of the river, pointed
    Towards rut, casting
Their passion out. Weeping philosopher,
They re-affirm the world,
    The stars by which they ran,
Now this precise place holds them
Again. They reach the churning wall
Of the brute waterfall that shed
Them young from its cauldron pool.
    A hundred times
    They lunge and strike

Against the hurdles of the rock ;
Though hammering water
    Beats them back
Still their desire will not break.
They coil and whip and kick,
    Tensile for their truth's
Sake ; give to the miracle
Of their treadmill leaping
The illusion of the natural.

The present in torrential flow
    Nurtures its own
    Long undertow :

They work it, strike and streak again,
Filaments in suspense.
　　The lost past shoots them
Into flight out of their element
In bright transilient sickle-blades
　　Of light ; until upon
The instant's height of their inheritance
They chance in descant over the loud
Diapasons of flood, jack out of reach
And snatch of clawing water,
　　　Stretch and soar
　　　Into easy rapids

Beyond, into half-haven, jounce over
Shelves upstream ; and know no question
　　But, pressed by their cold blood,
Glance through the known maze.
They unravel the thread to source
　　To die at their ancestry's
Last knot, knowing no question.
They meet under hazel trees
Are chosen and so mate. In shallows as
The stream slides clear, yet shirred
　　　With broken surface where
　　　Stones trap the creamy stars

Of air, she scoops at gravel with fine
Thrust of her exact, blind tail ;
        At last her lust
Gapes in a gush on her stone nest
And his great squanderous peak
        Shudders his final hunger
On her milk ; seed laid on seed
In spunk of liquid silk.
So in exhausted saraband their slack
Convulsions wind and wend galactic
        Seed in seed, a found
        World without end.

The circle's set, proportion
Stands complete and,
        Ready for death,
Haggard they hang in aftermath
Abundance, ripe for the world's
        Rich night, the spear.
Why does this fasting fish
So haunt me ? Gautama, was it this
You saw from river-bank
At Uruvela ? Was this
        Your glimpse
        Of holy law ?

23. *Elizabeth Hardwick*

Not content with having had four husbands, she
Built her own monument in masonry.
Children were incidental to the grand design
With which she hoped to perpetuate her line.
From four-quartered England she quarried stone
And stamped upon this hill her seal of bone,
This house at Hardwick, perfect in proportion,
Such faultless symmetry her heart's vocation.
Day after day she stood, stiff in brocaded age,
Scaffolding the sky with an architect's outrage,
Cursed and cuffed her masons, when water froze
Mixed mortar with beer and still the great walls rose ;
Caught a cold, standing in bitter frost,
Her own death merely an item of the cost.
Elizabeth Hardwick, four times married,
Bess behind your back, as harridan-harried,
Your husbands stepped into their death vaults and
Opened their treasure chests for your white hand ;
Blood congealed to brick, heart bled to rock,
A pedigree more durable than human stock,
Upon these four-square summits raised your initials,
An eyrie of windows with your signed credentials.
Face to face with you, who could doubt your brave surmise,
Still staring from your thousand vigilant eyes.

24. *Kilvey Hill, Swansea*

Above the bay's sweep
the mass of mountain
sits towards the sea
like a dead mole.

Heather and bracken mottle
its tough skin green-brown.
I stub my toe
kicking its grass tufts.

What can this high hill tell me
more than twenty years
lived in this place, growing
away?

That there is something solid
about mountains.
You need faith
to make them move.

Kilvey Hill
sits seaward
six drizzling miles
from where I started.

25. *Teacher*

Something in the face describes.
Among the years of chalk and dinner
Duty, something like resignation.
                                A line
Around the edges of the mouth's smile
Charted in a hundred well-worn
Atlases, a graph become
Diagonal with the year's passing.
The eyes light up
The notches on the slope,
Memory rescores
A schoolboy's try for Wales, an
Oxford Scholarship.
                        The pencilled finger
Stiffens for an evening's
Marking among the detritus
Of paper.

26. *Rhondda Murder*

Statistics show
the sum of murders grows,
but do not count the tears
that furrow wretched faces
in places far enough away
to smooth a conscience crease, dispel fears.

We never thought to fear
a murder happening here :
we knew its horror sieved, not fully felt,
through screen killings, the front page spread,
like a child's idea of death,
something never dreamt of for himself.

What heart beat yesterday, today is still,
no ache, no joy, no hate, no love, no will.
A mother's heart breaks in her eyes,
a father's pain is gathered into rage,
and parents watch their children as they play
anxious while a frightened man hides.

27. *Two Love Poems*

I will not pluck you flowers
Let them live and bloom beautiful
and dim beside your vital loveliness.

I will not bring you birds in cages
Let the sky-cascades of birdsong
show how sweet your music is.

I will bring you love,
because I cannot help myself.

How big your eyes are
    my wide-afraid doe !
When I come too near
    they would have me go,
but it is your fear
    that incites me so !

28. *For My Grandmother*

For now I see the skull beneath the flesh,
The shape of the brittle bones, and the brown
Stains on knotted hands, that for ever pluck
At the hard, unyielding wood that rests her arm.

There is nothing left in her now ; her dreams
Have died, and her memory withers here.
She walks backwards in the drifting footprints
Of her life, and has forgotten all things

But the man she loved, and her childhood years,
Sorrow, and striving, and a little joy.
Hardly she breathes ; the slight fall of the sheet
Is the only witness of life I see.

Oh, do not go, do not leave me alone—
Mother and child, you are both ; I have no more,
And so I am selfish, wishing to keep
Even the empty frame to hold my love.

But you are not mine to hold. I shall lose
You at last to silence, and be alone :
And no longer being impatient, wish
That the burden of love had never thus been shed.

29. *Tryweryn*

'Nothing's gone that matters—a dozen farms,
A hollow of no great beauty, scabby sheep,
A gloomy Bethel and a field where sleep
A few dead peasants. There are finer charms
Observed in rising water, as its arms
Circle and meet above the walls ; in cheap
Power and growing profits. Who could reap
Harvests as rich as this in ploughmen's palms ?
All's for the best—rehoused, these natives, too,
Should bless us for sanitation and good health.
Later, from English cities, see the view
Misty with hiraeth—and their new-built wealth.'

'All of our wealth's in men—and their life's blood
Drawn from the land this water drowns in mud.'

30. *Folk Museum*

This house we build is quite correct,
Each stone numbered before removal,
The dry mud floor measured for texture.
The willow pattern is proper,
And the dark oak chest, and bread cage.
In such a room all of the generations choked to death
Find now no home.

Preserving, we clean out dirt,
Expel the worms, reduce their dampness down
To a mild, moist breeze,
And show our children round
This simulacrum of their grandsire's hearth.

Written on cards, the processes are here—
But not the touch ; the handle strange to the hand,
The cupboard stiff —at home, in our plastic world,
The story's quaint—until we spill salt,
Crack mirrors, see the moon
Virgin through glass—and then the empty house
Fills again, and behind the curtained panes
A hungry child dies stifled in foul air.

31. *Ann Griffiths*

In little time I stake my claim
To all the panoply of fame.
My words are air, their manuscript
Forgetful flesh, a bony crypt
To lay these stillborn creatures in.

This foolishness of light intent
I turn to praise, my patterns meant,
Poor gift, for Him by whose free gift
My life is bought ; the seasons sift
Away my youth, my fear, my sin.

The fire upon my hearth is tame,
God's gentle creature ; now my name
Is signed in polished oak and brass,
My soul is singing, clear as glass,
Pure as this babe I bear within.

My songs as light as ash are spent ;
My hope's elsewhere, a long descent
In flesh and land—and yet the air
Stirs with fresh music, calls me where
Intricate webs of words begin.

Lord, let me not be silent till
All earth is grinding in Your mill !

32. *Elegy for Llywelyn Humphries*

Liquor, wages, automobiles, women, dope—
your gang ran all the rackets in town.
Chicago your sweet moll, Al Capone your boss,
as in the old films with grin and gun
you swaggered through the glittering twenties.

This morning, picking up a magazine, I
happen to come across your obituary : death
at seventy-six in San Quentin hospital,
quietly, delivered by the cop cancer.
The photo shows you prosperous and gentle,

like a priest or grandfather, the scars
a boxer's perhaps but surely no killer's.
How strange then to discover that, in your day,
you swindled the state of a cool million,
sent your kid brother to the chair

and, these last years in the penitentiary,
read books on bees and economics ; still more,
that your family was known to be Welsh—
farmers from some remote and derelict bro
sweating for a new deal in America.

Ah, Llywelyn, you were one of us, man !
I recognise you now and all your crooked kind :
small timers, fugitives from your people's past,
you got on in the big-shot world, but
had to face that most solitary music in the end.

So take it easy when I can't help wondering
who you might have been, with a name like that
and such remarkable enterprise, if only
you had crowed here in your own back yard.
Druan, I mourn a hoodlum, my compatriot.

33. *Elegy for Seamus O'Halloran*

You were no rebel, but the man who sold
sticks and vinegar in our village when I was a boy ;
Irish, of course, with the blue eyes and bog-face
that belong to your breed, for us the only
Paddy who ever had the blarney and the brogue.

On the side of your low cart, there was
a shamrock in the peeling gold of Erin go Bragh ;
often, holding my mother's jug under the cask,
I used to wonder at those words, why
too the small, dark horse's name was Rosaleen.

Years later, at college by now, I remember
asking you to give us Kevin Barry in the voice
kept always for the exile's parlour ballads
that pleased our neighbours, and sold
your ramshackle wares by its emerald charm.

'Bejasus, that's no song for a gentleman !'
you said, as full pelt down the terrace
went the poor, lashed mare. 'Up the Republic !'
I shouted from our step, but you were gone
beyond my die-hard fury on the road to Rhydfelin.

We never saw you in our street again,
or else the tinker's wail and bell were silent
as you passed our door ; whatever, I was
glad to hear, soon afterwards, that you had left
the valley and were back, at last, in Donegal.

Today, I would shake your hand, Seamus ;
for, as much as Yeats and Pearse and Connolly,
(they are no strangers in my house)
you taught me this dear, green truth : who
sings, or bleeds, for his country is best at home.

34. *Supermarket*

Sometimes I think I would like a spell in prison
In a humane country, for a political offence ;
Somewhere where the library service is efficient,
Or Scandinavia, where wives come in at weekends.

But better still in nineteenth-century Russia
To be exiled from the capital with friends,
And between the talk and drink to write the scriptures
Of our blinding human future without end.

To live rough and die fighting is also an ideal
(Guevara testifies) not yet out of date,
Like the soft cities to the high sierra, our trivial
Existence to the life we contemplate,

And the peasant ways are comely whatever you say
About hardship and early death. Ripe apples are stored
For the winter, no visiting stranger pays
For his wine, and the year goes round as before.

Choosing identities in a mad supermarket
(O packaged metaphor, bring me to a decision)
Good poets go home and wryly dig the garden.
Sometimes I think I should like a spell in prison.

35. *The Lascars*

When I was a boy they came in blackness
from black ships together, gripping an unseen circle
protected from the pack of the crowd.

Lascars, my father would say,
they'll empty the pubs tonight,
—and we'd see them in Wind Street by tailors' windows
huddled together, left alone.

One Monday, the *Evening Post* said blood had been found
on the pavement across the road from Sidney Heath's,
so *Lascars* my father said, and I stopped writing homework,
feeling the deft slit of the knife.

Then I was looking at coats in the window,
a man at the edge of means, indifferent to the town,
aching to be away. Quietly
they ringed me, staring into the same tailor's window,
dark in their quietness, unsure of the strange town,
nudging each other like schoolboys, they giggled
and fingered the frayed collars of loose shirts.

And *Lascars* I thought, as my dead father tugged,
but they smiled at me shyly, turning
to walk down Wind Street
to their ship.

36. *Erratum : for R. S. Thomas*

In his sheep crud
grinning at broken walls and passing cars
or parrying the wind, hoeing
the chopped shales,
your stinking, central, universal man.

On the other side of arthritic oaks
they lay as momentary sleepers,
the same wind fluttering gingham,
cooling the damp skin,
and moved together.

They moved together
with the fox's slow lope,
the flap of big birds across the fields
flying to the high meadows,
and moved then with the quick beat
of small birds
feathered like the sun.

37. *To Catherine, Aged Two*

In nineteen forty-nine I climbed the wall
of an orchard, in the city where I was born,
and reached for a line of decorative shells
along the top.
Another line was shining there,
of green bottle-glass, and I watched
the strange flap open in my hand
where the first river was running
over the smooth cement.

Then I fell squealing to the floor
of the alley below the wall,
crying (I was a child), for my blood,
and the apples I had lost.

I have no faith that words
will live through fire.
Bombs will bewilder poetry.
But like the old man at his net
we saw this summer (whom you forget)
I mend these holes with thread

which tears as easily as weed
against the rock.
Like water as he drew,
love will not hold and come
to the sweep of cast words
in any bay,
though something's caught
in the swell, and the patient haul

of syllables through wrack
towards the boat.
What's a girl to know of this ?
A puritan who sings his trial,
plucking white feathers
from the winter's
arching wings.

Two years have advanced
in my retreat. Yet trounced
in all significance by you
and rendered suspect by your joy,
I am the tool of all
your confidence and will.
Twenty-four months in sum
is everything. Flood,
fire, and laying on of hands.
My wound is yours, for love,
my pain a benediction for your use.

The broken toy demands repair.
Daddy, mend it. I wind the cellotape
and tie the threads until
there is a dog again.
You lose your cushion.
Daddy, find it. So I crawl
beneath your sister's crib
and grasp the thing.
Such clarity will bring
existence to its knees

and pleading to be essence.
The temple veil is rent—
but *Daddy mend it.*

This woman, in her time,
was sluggish to the task.
We broke the night for birth
but lost the day, and still
she pressed for freedom.
Your mother had become
a wrenching muscle and a cry.
He said, *I'll have to cut her*—
offering the phrase for me
to cut my teeth on.
I waved my hand so casually
you'd think I was concealing pride
for some high honour,
that with his knife her blood
would flow in every vein
and from her womb the child unlocked
would sing all joy.

But when the lift was closed
and they were gone,
there was no sign.
I was no Abraham.
I could not write a word on sterile walls,

for love betrays its dream of power.
Will *Daddy mend it* ?
If he can.
Know impotence is shared
by all men in their strength,
who love whatever lives
so excellently made.
Your body is delight,
and pity too, and fear,
though while you kick your limbs
all debts are paid.

All substance shapes itself
and blood is free.
I have no wisdom for *your* wound,
if wound there be.
Take what you can, while I
may give and make,
there's no diminishing
love's shoreless lake.
And when you must observe
the weakness I must show—
then mend it, too.

38. *The Grave*

I pass your grave
Daily ; walk up and down
On it. I know that under
The bright grass there is nothing
But your dry bones. Prytherch,
They won't believe that this
Is the truth. Rumours start
Like hill fires ; empty minds
Blow on them. Someone has seen
You at a meeting ; somewhere
A bomb grumbles. Echoes
Reverberate in the heart's
Hollows. Durable
As a tree in history's
Landscape, you are renewed
By wishes, by foliage
Of young hopes . . .
                        It is the old
Failing, a skirmish seen
As a battle, victory turned
To a legend before it is won.

39. *Ynys Enlli*

Is it a reminder ?
Is this why the sea leaves it
Unsubmerged ? Tirelessly it repeats
Itself or re-arranges
Its outlines. Under the grass
Are the choirs of dead men.

On mornings that are too cruel
To believe in, it gives itself
To its fasts, to the flagellations
Of spray ; suffering also
The bleakness of the seal's stare.

Sorrowfully the spirit
Inspects it. Its one tree
Is the cross, that a saint's hand
Planted ; a lavatory now
For the starlings that have their roost there.

40. *On My Fortieth Birthday*

When I was forty the stocktaker came
to take stock. He was dressed in black
like that old advertisement for Sandeman's port.
Let me see your books, he said.
I blew the dust off my ledgers
and showed him the blank pages.
These are nothing but blank pages, he said.
Are you trying to be whimsical ?
He had the flat voice that BBC announcers use
when they describe calamity.
My plans are still maturing, I said,
I am on the point of doing something important.
An old lady in Port Talbot likes two of my poems
and she's ordered two copies for the library.
I am piling my rubbish against oblivion,
stacking it against the dark.
If you go up to Aberystwyth
you'll find my name misspelt in the dust.

He looked at me in contempt
right through to the lack of backbone.
Yes, he said, but what have you done ?
What have you actually done with your lovely life ?
Well, I said, it's like this . . .
I groped for the cudgelled album
where the corpses were kept.

Outside was the switchyard, with the expresses
coming at one another from all directions.
I hadn't heard a bird around here for years.
Loneliness came down like a lid.

I'll be back, old Sandeman said,
you'd better get those pages filled . . .

41. *Cwmtaf Bridge*

(For Penri Williams)

It's fifteen years since we had a summer so dry
That the bridge at Cwmtaf rose to human eye
Above the reservoir water, and they say, before
That, it hadn't been seen for fifteen years more.
We made our way to it across the dried mud
And in a quiet evening of July we stood
On the loosened stonework, watched the fish rise
Breaking the level water, snapping at gnats and flies.
From the crumbled parapet a couple of night lines were out,
Somebody hoping to catch an illegal trout.
And we traced the line of a road coming down to the river
And talked of things that are gone now forever
Under the reservoir, how the bridge in the old days
Was the meeting place of all the country ways
For flirting and fighting or just spitting in the stream,
And how old people's memories are no more than a dream.
And as we savoured the cool evening calm
You told me the names and families of every farm
Whose ghostly rubble glimmered above the river banks
Where the pinetrees marshalled their mathematical ranks.
In the last light a buzzard hovered on outstretched wings
Over the dead homes where nobody sows or sings.
Far distant, it seemed, occasional traffic went by,
The water ar our feet mirrored the darkening sky,
Down to the dam's hard outline stretching away,
A lake of hushed twilight, pearl and silver-grey—

The bounty of nature harnessed for the works of man.
We could see down the valley to the tip above Aberfan.
We stayed there a long time, not talking much aloud.
The evening, the lake, the hills, were suddenly a shroud.

42. Cywydd o Fawl

(i Gyngor y Celfyddydau yn null y gogogynfeirdd a gogo)

Flap we our lips, praise Big Man,
Bards religious shire Cardigan.
Not frogs croaking are we
Not vain crows are bards tidy.
Wise is our speak, like Shadrach,
Hearken you now, people bach.
Mouth some, Cardiff ach y fi,
Not holy like Aberteifi.
Twp it is to speech so,
In Cardiff is gold yellow,
Truth it is and no fable,
All for bards respectable.
White Jesus bach, let no ill
Befall Big Heads Arts Council.
Pounds they have, many thousand,
Like full till shop draper grand.
Good is the work they are at,
Soaped they shall be in Seiat,
Reserved shall be for them
A place in Big Seat Salem.
Praised let them be for this thing,
Money they are disbributing
Like Beibil Moses his manna,
Tongue we all, bards Welsh, Ta !

43. *A Vision of the South Wales Coalfield*

I

I came down from the mountain where the red rose
struggled darkly ; walked the valley floor
through stacks of twisted metal that would impose
a pattern on my mind. This was the spoor

of Pity I had come to track. Certain now
of that feeling (always it came at twilight)
I searched to find the Beast, somewhere it lay low,
raged anger spent like money during flight.

There is a kind of passive violence
which moved me to this ; participation
through thought, only, like angst, as tense
as that, like land's dark mutation.

I found the place was filled with mine shafts deep.
The Beast lay there. I know. I heard it weep.

II

Blaenrhondda's hills are humps, big as night
and dark as cancer. Dawn curls slowly over
them until the high sun spews its light,
the quick forged strips like brass, dense colour

of amber. Memory recalls the struck pavement,
echo of hob-nailed feet, jocular voices in
the morning air recede ; the enslavement
of flesh by fire, by water, blue scarred skin

of silicotic men. While concepts—laws
of profit and the loss are played, the game
begins to pall. The huge Beast weakens, its claws
taunt only darkness, yet cast still with Cain.

Deep in one desolate and lonely mine
it lies, in base and tragic symbol of its time.

44.   *The Long Way Home*

Odysseus knew where he was going ;
He of all Greeks had the cunning
To steer a chancey course, make it safe
To take things as they come ; no half
Measures here ; what was offered he took
Of love, war and sea. Strange the book
Doesn't tell why such a man travelled
So far before he unravelled
The flax, made it to Ithaca.

45.   *Andromache*

Was it really like this ?
Was it enough to stand by
Talking of a noble love
To set against Helen's crooked eye,

Her easy passions ?
To let Cassandra's blind words
Float by on the night air
Like unseen birds ?

Playing the colonel's wife,
Always saying the right thing
At the right time, ignoring
The drum's dull pulsing

Even when your blood
Said otherwise under the rough
thrust of Ajax's hands.
Was this the stuff

Your dreams were made on ?
Was this how it had to be,
Fumbled by a stranger
Whilst Hector, he

Who put Troy before
His wife, looked on ?
You knew then how Helen felt
With Paris, or any man,

And yet said nothing
But what you should.
Was it then you knew
You wanted Hector dead ?

DIAL-A-POEM

1. *Not Worth the Record*

What is it that you expect, caller ?
Another voice of aloneness
In a different register, agreeing
Only in dischord, so that the scale
Cracks, sharps and flats mobbing
The instinctive harmonies ?
I am alone but not your ally,
A singer but in no mode of yours,
By my own fault poor and not
Your mobster, a failure in such sort
That all despair can use
Is the name, the notion of it, not
The feel, the pump of the gland,
The genital misdirection
Of fond secretions or the glass
Up, scrawny finger-held, aerating
The idioms of the blood.

You want to be sure of my failure
As the excommunicate prod
And identify the curse ?
Herein I cannot help you
Evidentially, for what I know
Is ignorance. Hard by the pillar
I willed down evil and my hand
Pulled back. I quartered the nave
Sniggering and the shearling choir
Climbed to a paean over-

Towering it. What I have willed
Has rarely happened, just
As rarely as beneficence
Was my full choice. How can I
Offer this failure to you
For identification, caller ?
And how persuade your truculence
That I no longer will it
Otherwise ?

2. *Deerhound*

There are no deerhounds in Wales—
Or perhaps one ; in Cardiff, loping
On an elegant lead in Llandaff Fields,
Exotic in Queen Street, posing
For photographs. But there are
No true deerhounds. Our fat corgis
Sit irritably in English country houses,
Our loyal collies starve
Behind the doors of roadless farms.

But we parade our terriers. Square
And bristling, the brisk wire-
haired fox terrier, the Welsh terrier
Indigenous black and tan, thin
Scars on heads and legs like a collier,
We like these dogs. I knew one
Curl herself over a drunk man's heart
On a moor filling with blizzard.
They grin at death with their teeth.

I would have a deerhound coloured
Slippery as charcoal, running
Tactfully at the edge of eyesight,
Soft as dust after his great quarry.
Once back of the ruined hills I saw
A fabulous hare living on grass
Too small for sheep, thrusting
Through coal-spoil. He leapt
In my sleep for months.

With such small deer my hound
Would not soil his slobber.
In darkness, on the edge of terror,
He would run, he would run loose
And noiseless. Black as night-fur, kicking
Into the black, what antlered
Game he would rip at, what
Terrible beasts drag back
Alive for my keeping.

3. *Dial-a-Poem*

You are listening to a recorded message
For that's what poems are.
It's no good expecting
Even the *Readers' Digest* version
Of *Paradise Lost*
For the price of a local call
Even supposing you've lost your paradise :

So whoever's listening now,
Tom, Dick or Jerry, Mary, Joan or Mary Jane,
Or whatever name you're phoning under,
At the third stroke it will be
Whatever your age is precisely.
You will find from the instructions
On the appropriate circular that charges
Are reversible, but not ages.

Through your receiver you are now in touch
With stolen property, for a poet claims
As his own anything he can lay words on.
He will tell tales overheard in public bars,
Private beds and nationalised boardrooms
Given that they are common property,
Given that they spell sense
In the human heart's directory.

At the third stroke you will not be alone
In your listening. I am putting you through

To the extension you asked for
Without your having spoken. Someone
Somewhere would like to hear from you :
So dial yourself and talk of what you've known
In words that are musical,
In rhythms that remember
Or explore tomorrow,
For that's what poems are.
You are listening to a recorded message.

The weather in the Bristol Channel area
From six p.m. this evening will be
Whatever it will be ; and all roads
To an easy answer to the simplest question
Are treacherous as usual.

This is your alarm call, though
To-day is not the day
When on the third stroke
It will be death o'clock precisely :
On that day you cannot pay for further time,
You are cut off and can't be re-connected.
Please use the yellow pages of your laughter :
They are at the back of your life's book.

You are listening to a recorded

4. *Aspects of Now*

The moment is now
you can test it all by now
by how things are now.

There can't be any other moment
though now would seem to be surrounded
by future contemporary and past,
the parts of a verb, a way of saying.

No, it's all here now, so judge it
now you have it, now. I am part of it
for you and you for me since
you are listening. Listen to now.

Now for this world faltering
from growth to fission. For Wales too
in its greenness and intimacy, from
the bowelled smoke of the South to
the sliced stone of the North. Now
with some valleys drowned and some still human,
with a drover still living and buses
that cross the sea, with more trees

than sheep, with a language still alive now
which to our shame I'm not using now.
This is the moment to hold these things
in balance, to decide now which way

to allow or leash instinct, to tip
what we have into the scales now
knowing that now is the golden age
the only moment worth having. The now

if you like when I've stopped talking and
you're alone with now or with your lover
or friends or sheep or family or fellow
demonstrators or the long rising pavement

or rain on the hills of Wales, the smear
of light from a bus window, any now
is infinite space, is everything, is whatever
you and it and they are. Now you have it.

Today has it all, sunshine,
snow to the north, the lake
frozen over, the Sunday leisure
of friends, a silence like

a seizing up of the megamachine,
a forgetting of towns.
Broken pieces of ice skipped
over ice sing no tunes

but hit one high sweet note
each time they touch the ice,
hold the note to its twittering death
halfway over the lake. Wild geese

are frozen in attitudes, improbably
secure from the fowler. Nothing forages.
Five of us and a happy dog
alone now on the crisp ridges.

The barrowed dead live for us,
we banish fear of raucous change
to this lake, this moorland, this
Wales, dismiss the sly danger

in laughter, love, attention
to now, as given us by all
our senses, the sight, the sound,
the feel, the taste, the ice-sweet smell

of a cerulean winter's day
on water, skin and grass
now we are together and absolute
in this moment of grace.

5. Dial a Poem

Dial a poem. Dial a song.
Dial a comfort when love goes wrong.
Dial a peace when the soldiers cry war.
Dial a crust when the wolf's at the door.
Dial a pint when you're looking for ale.
Dial success when you're starting to fail.
Dial a dawn when the night is too long.
Dial a poem. Dial a song.

I dialled my love and she listened to me,
I said I'd be true till the fish left the sea,
I vowed that I'd love her till gold turned to brass,
And springtime forgot to replenish the grass,
I said that I'd love her, for passion like mine
Was purer than Sunday and truer than wine.

But love it is fickle, and love is a flower,
And love very often lasts only an hour,
And lovers who swear with their hand on their heart
That nothing will change them, how quickly they part.

Dial a poem. Dial a song.
Dial a comfort when love goes wrong.
Dial a pint when you're looking for ale.
Dial for youth when you're starting to fail.

I dialled a new love instead of the old,
And vowed that I'd love her till brass turned to gold,
And I took her to church while my heart was aflame,
And swore I'd abandon the bachelor game,
And we made us a baby to bounce on our knee,
And said we'd be true till the fish left the sea,
Till the fish left the sea and till yellow turned red,
I vowed I'd be true to the girl that I'd wed.

But love it is fickle, and love is a flower,
And love very often lasts only an hour,
And the lovers who swear with their hand on their heart
That nothing will change them, how quickly they part.

I dialled a new love instead of the old,
And vowed that I'd love her till brass turned to gold,
But I had a crossed line, so I put down the phone,
And when I tried next found no dialling tone.

Dial a marriage. Dial a joy.
Dial a girl and dial a boy.
Dial a ribbon. Dial a swing.
Dial an answer for everything.
Dial a pint when you're looking for ale.
Dial a strength when you're starting to fail.
Dial a wife who knows what you are.
Dial a moon and dial a star.
Dial a night when the day is too long.
Dial a poem. Dial a song.

NOTES ON CONTRIBUTORS

Reverend EUROS BOWEN was born at Treorci and educated at U.C.W. Aberystwyth and St. Catherine's College, Oxford. He has published four books of poetry and is Rector of Llangywair, near Bala.

DAVID CHARLES was born in Denbighshire and educated at U.C.W. Aberystwyth. He taught and lectured in North Wales and is at present a County Inspector of Schools.

TONY CURTIS was born in Carmarthen, educated at the Queen Elizabeth Grammar school there and in Greenhill Comprehensive, Tenby. He has just completed a postgraduate course at University College, Swansea.

ELWYN DAVIES teaches in the International Quaker School just outside Utrecht. He has recently had a collection of poems, *Words Across the Water*, published by Christopher Davies.

RAYMOND GARLICK was born in London and educated at University College, Bangor. Teacher and poet, he is now Senior Lecturer in Trinity College, Carmarthen. His last book, *An Introduction to Anglo-Welsh Literature,* has just been published by the University of Wales Press.

EMYR HUMPHREYS is well known as a novelist. He now lectures in Drama at University College, Bangor. His book of poems, *Ancestor Worship,* was published this year by Gwasg Gee.

ROBERT HUNTER was born in Liverpool and educated at the University and School of Art there. Teacher and artist, he is Head of the Art Department, Trinity College, Carmarthen.

BRAMWELL JONES studied at Coleg Harlech and at University College, Cardiff. He is now teaching in Thurrock Technical College, Essex.

ROLAND MATHIAS was a Headmaster of schools in Pembroke, Derbyshire and Birmingham. Poet, writer and editor, he now lives in Brecon.

LESLIE NORRIS jas just edited the Memorial Volume of essays on Vernon Watkins published by Faber. The Triskel Press published a collection of poems, *The Long Winter*, and Chatto has recently published another collection, *Ransoms*.

JOHN ORMOND was born in Dunvant and after years as a journalist he is now a director and producer of films. His book of poems, *Requiem and Celebration*, was published by Christopher Davies last year.

DOUGLAS PHILLIPS was educated at Queen Elizabeth School, Carmarthen and Wadham College, Oxford. He now lectures in English at Derby College of Technology.

JOHN POOK was educated at Gowerton and Cambridge and is now a lecturer in English at Pagdate College of Education.

JOHN RICHARDSON was born and educated in the Rhondda and is now a student at Trinity College, Carmarthen.

SALLY ROBERTS was born in London and educated at University College, Bangor. Her book of poems, *Turning Away,* was published by Gwasg Gomer last year.

MEIC STEPHENS is Editor of *Poetry Wales* and Assistant Director (Literature) of the Welsh Arts Council. He was a co-editor of the anthology *The Lilting House* published by Dent/Davies.

NED THOMAS taught English at the University of Salamanca and in Moscow. He is joining the staff of the English Department of U.C.W. Aberystwyth in October and is editing the new magazine *Planet*.

PETER THOMAS was born in Manchester and educated at University College, Cardiff. He now teaches in New Brunswick.

R. S. THOMAS is at present Vicar of the parish of Aberdaron, North Wales. His poetry is read in all parts of the Western world.

JOHN TRIPP is a free-lance writer and broadcaster living in Cardiff. His collection of poems, *The Loss of Ancestry*, was published by Christopher Davies last year.

HARRI WEBB was educated at Magdalen College, Oxford and is chief librarian at Mountain Ash. His book of poems, *The Green Desert*, was published by Gwasg Gomer last year.

EVAN GWYN WILLIAMS was born in Glyneath and educated at Coleg Harlech. He is now working in Swansea.

JOHN STUART WILLIAMS is Head of the Department of English and Drama at the College of Education, Cardiff. His book of poems, *The Green Rain*, was published by Christopher Davies and he was the co-editor of *The Lilting House* published by Dent/Davies.

GWYN WILLIAMS, well known for his books *The Burning Tree* and *An Introduction to Welsh Poetry*, now lives near Aberystwyth. His collection of poems, *The Inns of Love*, was recently published by Christopher Davies.

HERBERT WILLIAMS was born at Aberystwyth and is now a journalist with the *South Wales Echo*. His book of poems, *The Trophy*, was published by Christopher Davies in 1968.